Patti Smith
Horses, Paris 1976

Claude Gassian

Patti Smith
Horses, Paris 1976
Claude Gassian

Abrams, New York

Paris 1976

On November 10, 1975, the anniversary of the passing of Arthur Rimbaud, my first album, *Horses*, was released on Arista Records. I remember walking down the street with Lenny Kaye, seeing it for the first time in the window of a record store in Greenwich Village. We had no idea how it would be received in the world but were thrilled when offered a tour in Europe. I was especially excited to perform in Paris. I had already visited the city twice, as a young stranger. In the spring of 1969, my sister Linda and I happily wandered the city of cafes, Juliette Gréco, Jean Genet, *Breathless*, and Jacques Rivette. I returned to Paris alone in late October of 1973, tracing the footsteps of the ghost of Rimbaud.

On a spring morning in 1976, filled with joyful anticipation, my band arrived at Le Bourget airport. Lenny Kaye, Richard Sohl, Ivan Kral, and Jay Dee Daugherty, our small crew, and manager Jane Friedman were greeted by Jean-Noël Ogouz, a calm and supportive representative from our record company. My beloved pianist, Richard Sohl, and I were in a car with Claude Gassian, an energetic and amiable photographer. I was wearing dark glasses, a black silk dress, and a men's Saint Laurent jacket. I felt like a character in another kind of *Don't Look Back*, slightly arrogant yet filled with hidden excitement. Paris in my mind was much more than a tour stop or a night of communion through rock 'n' roll. It had somewhat formed me: the clothes I wore, the poetry I cherished, the movies that inspired me. After years of devouring French culture, I now had a chance to bring my own work to my cherished city.

On show day Jean-Noël and Claude accompanied me to Père-Lachaise cemetery to visit Jim Morrison's grave. There was no headstone for him, but the surrounding ones were covered with his lyrics written in chalk by young admirers. In a sense, they were his true headstones, created by those who loved him as a poet as well as a rock 'n' roll star. We paid homage to Jim Morrison and some of the great artists at rest: Proust, Oscar Wilde, Edith Piaf, Gerard de Nerval, and Delacroix. It was meaningful to visit Jim Morrison, as *Horses* included the song "Break it Up", my dream of him as a Promethean angel, written with Tom Verlaine.

On May 13, 1976, we played at Élysée Montmartre, after an interview with Philippe Manœuvre. I read from Jim Morrison's *An American Prayer* and exchanged feedback on my Duo Sonic with Lenny on his Stratocaster. The concert was raucous, the power of music binding us all. The young gathered around us in the streets. A kid named Alain Lahana, an acquaintance of the opening act, Bijou, had hitchhiked from Toulouse to see the concert. Years later he would become our French agent and dear friend, a wonderful twist of fate.

Before leaving Paris, at the Pathé Marconi office, Lenny and I proudly accepted *Horses*'s first and greatest accolade—the Charles Cros Award.

The band returned to Paris in October. Shortly after our arrival, we walked the rainy cobbled streets surrounding our concert venue, Pavillon de Paris, once an old slaughterhouse. We were opened by John Cale, who had produced *Horses*. So much happy anarchy as we raised our guitars and trounced "My Generation" while Jay Dee destroyed the drums. Backstage I was happy to spend time with Nico against a photomontage backdrop that felt like another century.

On October 20th, the birthday of Rimbaud, the band flew to Barcelona for a job in old but massive ice-skating rink. We returned to Paris in the morning, and that night we played at Le Bus

Palladium, a packed punk-rock club. Kids broke through the ceiling; the electricity went out and chaos erupted. But nothing could stop us, and we performed "Gloria" with Lenny and Ivan on acoustic guitars. For those crazy blessed moments, Paris belonged to us.

Claude, Jean-Noël, Alain Dister, and I ended our time together in Place des Vosges. I saw the house where Victor Hugo lived and the desk where he wrote. As the afternoon passed, I was just by myself building sandcastles with a small girl I thought I'd never see again. *She is the future*, I remember thinking.

The miracle of an envelope of negatives brings these moments back to me. They capture a glimpse of the highly charged atmosphere of 1976 and the joyful hubris of a rock 'n' roll band. Images of my sunglasses, boxing boots, tattered Rastafarian T-shirt. Shots of my band that produce both pleasure and sorrow. Our guitarist and bass player, Ivan Kral, a refugee from Prague, died in 2020. Our incomparable pianist, Richard Sohl, died suddenly of heart failure in 1990. Our friend Nico also departed. But back then they were all very much alive. A bit wild, tramping from city to city, greeting the people. A slideshow of black-and-white images generating so many emotions, the greatest being gratitude. Thank you, Claude Gassian.

—Patti Smith, March 2025

June 1975

I was on my first trip to New York!

The Rolling Stones were getting ready for a series of six straight concerts at Madison Square Garden. I didn't miss a single one. And I came away with some fabulous shots of the band on stage, as always with them.

It was hard to imagine that just a few blocks away, at Electric Lady Studios, a young woman was recording a debut album that would spark a fire and reshape the entire landscape of rock music and songwriting—which, by the mid-1970s, was starting to run out of steam.

Horses was released on November 10 by Arista Records. I knew Jean-Noël Ogouz, who represented the label in Paris, and I was in his office one day when he handed me this album by an unknown artist and told me I had to listen to it—*now.*

It had a minimalist black-and-white cover. Already a visual jolt. Shot by a photographer named Robert Mapplethorpe, the head-on portrait of Patti Smith—an unconventional beauty, androgynous and singular, with a steady gaze—seemed to signal something new, something dangerous.

From my very first listen, the album blew me away. The way she sang, the way she ran through the lyrics in an electric frenzy . . . It never left my side that whole year. I was obsessed with *Horses* and dreamed of meeting the musician behind it. My wish came true when Jean-Noël took me with him to the Bourget Airport to welcome her and her band on their arrival in Paris for her first concerts in France and the launch of the album.

I was finally going to photograph her.

She wanted to visit Jim Morrison's grave at Père-Lachaise Cemetery. It was a powerfully intense moment that I captured and took in in silence. Then, just before leaving, I asked her to pose for a few photos on a stone bench, a bit off to the side. She agreed. I caught her glances, her gestures . . . These were some of my first truly personal shots, my first trophies!

Up until then, I had rarely had such open access to the artists I'd covered—the ability to follow them from place to place, without having to watch the clock. This freedom taught me how to compose and to frame, but also to keep my distance, to know when to hold back and choose the right moment.

I was beginning to find my photographic voice.

After that first impromptu meeting, I felt like I'd been admitted to her inner circle, and I continued to follow her over the years during her visits to Paris.

What a surprise it was to revisit my old photos and rediscover this set from 1976. So many shots I'd forgotten, as well as some I'd never seen, which had never before been published.

I think we were all in love with her, in our own way.

And my photos were like stolen kisses . . .

—Claude Gassian, March 2025

On a spring morning in 1976 . . .

In a car . . .

. . . to Père-Lachaise cemetery . . .

. . . to visit Jim Morrison's grave.

On show day . . .

The interview.

On May 13, 1976, we played at Élysée Montmartre . . .

```
Setlist
Early show (6:30 p.m.)

1. We're Gonna Have a Real Good Time Together
(The Velvet Underground)
2. Kimberly (Patti Smith)
3. Redondo Beach (Patti Smith)
4. Free Money (Patti Smith)
5. Privilege (Set Me Free)
6. Pissing in a River
7. Pumping (My Heart)
8. Ain't It Strange
9. An American Prayer (Jim Morrison / The Doors)
10. Radio Ethiopia
11. Land / Gloria

Encore:
12. My Generation (The Who)


Late show (9:00 p.m.)

1. We're Gonna Have a Real Good Time Together
(The Velvet Underground)
2. Kimberly (Patti Smith)
3. Redondo Beach (Patti Smith)
4. Free Money (Patti Smith)
5. Privilege (Set Me Free)
6. Pissing in a River
7. Pumping (My Heart)
8. Ain't It Strange
9. Radio Ethiopia
10. Land / Gloria
11. Time Is On My Side (Norman Meade)

Encore:
12. My Generation (The Who)
```

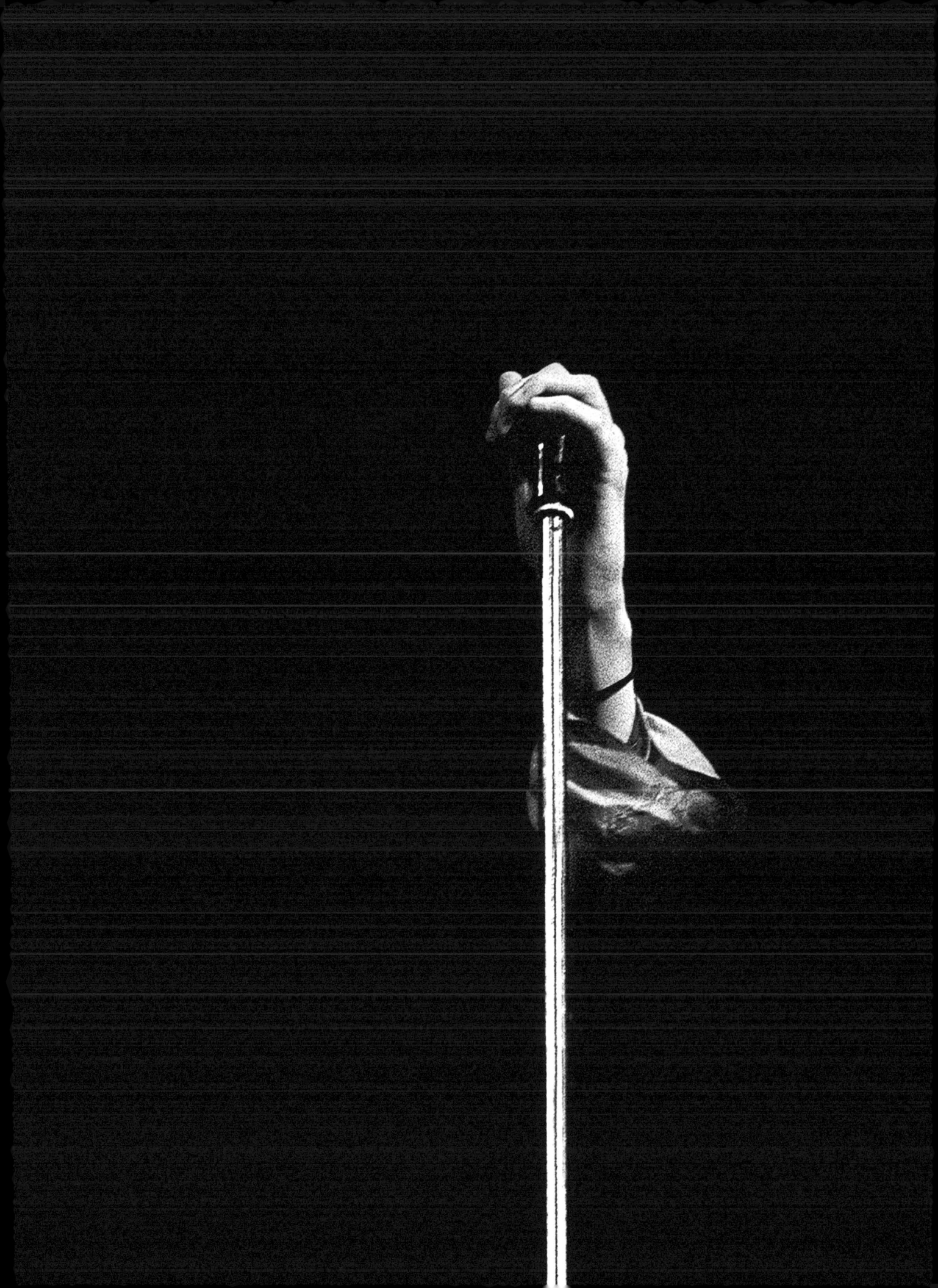

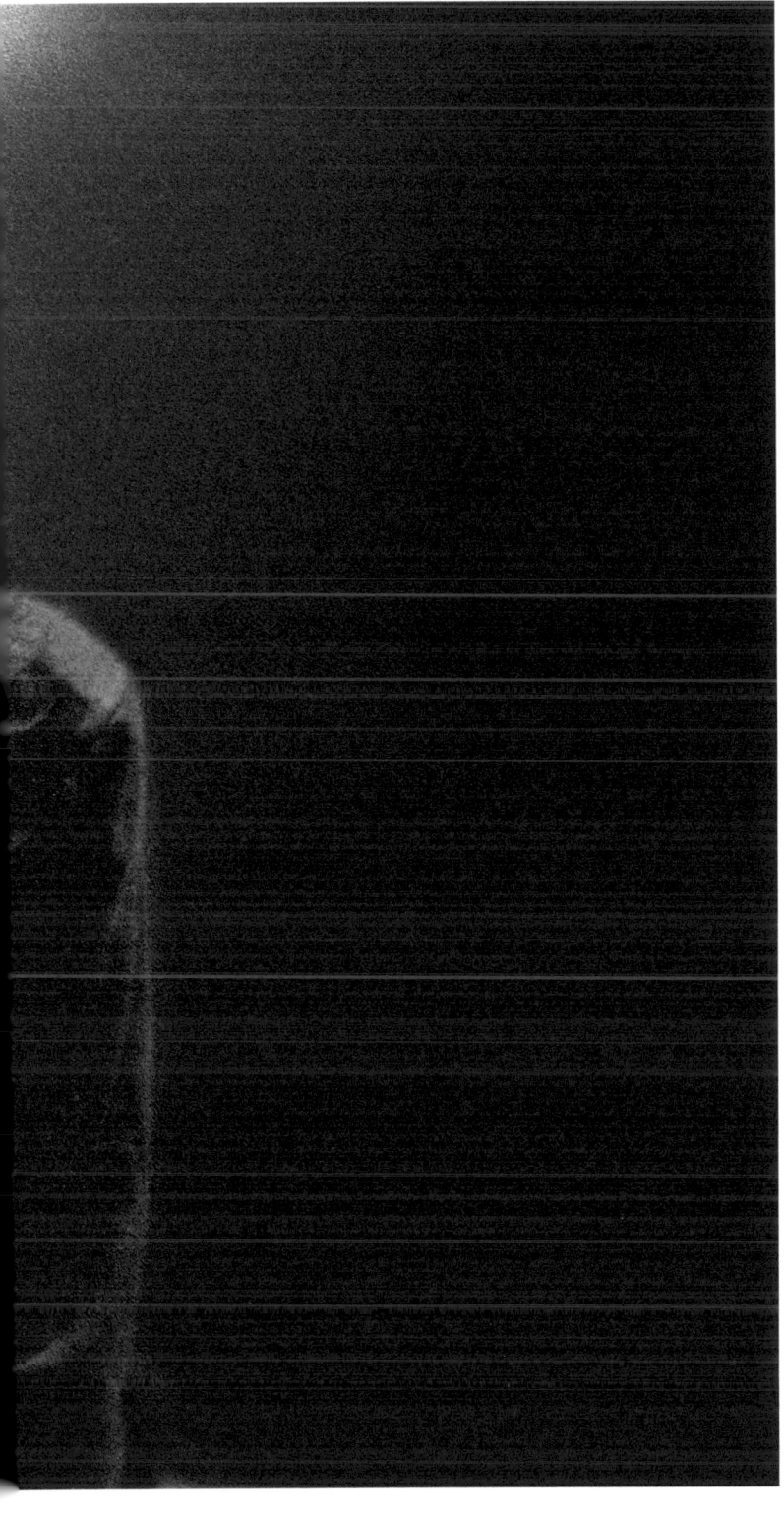

Horses's *first and greatest accolade.*

ACADEMIE CHARLES CROS

Pop Music . Patti Smith . Horses

GRAND PRIX DU DISQUE

We walked the rainy cobbled streets . . .

October,
Pavillon de Paris,
backstage . . .

With John Cale,
who produced Horses,
and Jane Friedman.

With Nico.

Pavillon de Paris,
October 19, 1976

Setlist

1. We're Gonna Have a Real Good Time Together
(The Velvet Underground)
2. Kimberly
3. Redondo Beach
4. Free Money
5. Pale Blue Eyes (The Velvet Underground)
6. Louie Louie (Richard Berry)
7. Ask the Angels
8. Time Is on My Side (Norman Meade)
9. Pumping (My Heart)
10. Ain't It Strange
11. Radio Ethiopia
12. Rock 'N' Roll N*****
13. Gloria
14. Land
15. My Generation (The Who)

For those crazy, blessed moments, Paris belonged to us . . .

We ended our time together
in Place des Vosges.

To Nicole, Chloé, and Lila Gassian. And to Vartoui as well.

Acknowledgments

Sincere thanks to Patti Smith for her collaboration and enthusiasm.

Special thanks to Jean-Noël Ogouz, for believing in me from the start; you left us too soon. This book is for you.

My thanks also to Alain Lahana, for your thoughtful, guiding hand.
Antoine Leroux-Dhuys, for our conniving and Moriyama moments.
Véronique Beaufils, for your support and wise advice.
Olivier Fau, for your first impressions.
Marie Malvoisin, for your welcome perspective.
Richard Schroeder, for decades of sharing in music and pictures.
Patrice Demailly, for your careful retouching.
Marc Lumbroso
The Gallimard team: Giovanna, Nathalie, Anne, Martin, Amélie, Béatrice and Laetitia, Mathilde and Coline.

. . . and the little girl from the sandbox!

Claude Gassian and Patti Smith,
Paris, 1976

For Abrams:
Editor: Holly Dolce
Design Manager: Darilyn Lowe Carnes
Managing Editor: Amy Vinchesi
Production Manager: Larry Pekarek

Art Direction: Claude Gassian
Layout: Antoine Leroux-Dhuys
Copyediting: Nicole Tarbouriech
Image Processing: Marie Malvoisin

For Editions Gallimard:
Editorial: Nathalie Bailleux, Editorial Director; Giovanna Citi-Hebey,
Editorial Manager; Natércia Pauty, Department Assistant; Katia de
Azevedo, Text Preparation and Editing
Art Direction: Anne Lagarrigue, Art Director; Pascal Guédin, Illustrated
Books Coordinator
Production: Amélie Airiau, Head of Production
Press Office: Béatrice Foti, assisted by Laetitia Copin
Co-publishing: Mathilde Barrois, Head of International Co-Publishing,
assisted by Coline Briand

Library of Congress Control Number: 2025937203

ISBN: 978-1-4197-8974-8
eISBN: 979-8-89684-195-1

Printed and bound in Italy
10 9 8 7 6 5 4 3 2 1

Abrams books are available at special discounts when purchased
in quantity for premiums and promotions as well as fundraising or
educational use. Special editions can also be created to specification. For
details, contact specialsales@abramsbooks.com or the address below.

Abrams® is a registered trademark of Harry N. Abrams, Inc.

ABRAMS is represented in the UK and Europe by Abrams & Chronicle
Books, 1 West Smithfield, London EC1A 9JU and Média-Participations,
57 rue Gaston Tessier, 75166 Paris, France.
abramsandchronicle.co.uk and media-participations.com
info@abramsandchronicle.co.uk

ABRAMS The Art of Books
195 Broadway, New York, NY 10007
abramsbooks.com